Focus on

Thomas Hardy:
Poems of 1912–13

The 'Emma' Poems

John Greening

GREENWICH EXCHANGE
LONDON

Greenwich Exchange, London

Focus on
Thomas Hardy: *Poems of 1912-13*
© John Greening

First published in Great Britain in 2007
Reprinted 2012 and 2017

Printed and bound by imprintdigital.com
Cover design by December Publications
Tel: 07951511275

Greenwich Exchange Website: www.greenex.co.uk

Cataloguing in Publication Data is available
from the British Library

ISBN: 978-1-906075-04-0

Acknowledgements

My thanks to Helen Wood and the Indian King poets in Camelford for their creative company during the North Cornish passages; and Sally Searle of the Old Rectory, St Juliot, for her warm welcome to a dozen living poets.

Contents

Good Friday, St Juliot

March 1870,
drawing and measuring,
trying to rule a straight
line through those magic blue
eyes on his blue paper.

April, a century
later, and leaden skies
seal up St Juliot's
mortal remains. The rooks
preach resurrection, how

one thought it good to tear
down the original
home where they'd built their nests,
nave, chancel, ivy green
tower, whose inverted bells

never pealed, only tolled
passionate remedies,
desperate ends. He came
planning to lift the place
from its obscurity

into the modern age,
left with a pair of eyes
noticing how the slate
hid, beneath ransoms and
bluebells, unopened words.

John Greening

1

The Poetry

The present author can still recall a young maid he was fond of in his 'June time' emerging in tears from a tutorial where she had just been told that only half a dozen of Hardy's poems were any good. Like Philip Larkin, perhaps, she felt "that one reader at least would not wish Hardy's *Collected Poems* a single page shorter". We might not go as far as Larkin, but in the thirty years since that incident, F.R. Leavis' commandments have been largely forgotten and Hardy has emerged as the poet who has given English poetry its true bearings. Donald Davie was the critic to put us straight on the matter in *Thomas Hardy and British Poetry* (1973), emphasising his versatility as a prosodist, even while recognising certain limitations – nothing, surprisingly, to do with his pastoral subject matter, but rather a mechanical quality in the writing, a "cruel self-driving ... not the chip-chip of a mason's chisel, but a clank of iron girders swung down from a crane ..." Davie calls him "'a superb technician' who dismays us precisely by his *superbia*." Such accusations still lurk in the background when Hardy's poetry is discussed: he would write out his rhythmical lines and leave gaps to fill in the words later; he would use weird neologisms like 'existlessness' and 'day-dreamt'; he came to it too late, wrote too much and only because he had given up novels ...

It is true that he had given up novels by the time he wrote the *Poems of 1912–13*. But he had always been a poet, and some of his earliest pieces are the equal of (and indistinguishable from) those written in his eighties. By the time he resolved to be a full-time poet, when he was on his way to sixty, they had seen little but rejection. Florence Hardy's *Life,* in effect her husband's 'ghost-written' autobiography, quotes a typical review from an American journal, calling Hardy "a realistic novelist who ... has a grim determination to go down to posterity wearing the laurels of a poet", although in fact he had never ceased regarding poetry as the essence of literature: "At the risk of ruining all my worldly prospects I dabbled in it ... was forced out of it ... It came back upon me ... and there was never any 'grim determination'". Nor was it a matter of ambition, except to take his place in the 'Great Tradition', to (as the *Life* puts it) "have some poem or poems in a good anthology like the Golden Treasury".

What, then, are the qualities that have found the poems a steady readership long after other Victorians and Georgians have vanished? On the face of it, Hardy's poetry was ill-equipped for the 20th century and for the cry that in a difficult age poetry too must be difficult. Only a writer out of tune with the age would cling to Swinburne as one of his main influences, would choose to write in so audibly musical and instantly gratifying a style, telling stories, singing ballads, persisting in the impossible tradition of love poetry and lyric poetry even after the First World War. Didn't such a catastrophe demand a breaking and remaking of the art? Shouldn't poetry now find a fitting dissonance? Wasn't it the world that needed attending to, with its Great Powers, rather than Wessex and its sighing lovers? The one Victorian worthy to confront it was Hopkins, with his premonitory fractured style and his obscure cries of despair; or the American, Walt Whitman, already overcanopying mere English saplings; the only relevant Georgians were those prepared to write about the war. Free verse, imagism, surrealism, political chant and social outcry, dark immensities and deep personal rhythms were the appropriate style for a broken civilisation. What could a retired novelist from the mid-19th century have to say to the Eliot generation, the Auden generation?

Evidently a good deal, because the practitioners of this

new kind of verse recognised the enduring quality of Hardy's poetry, seeing for the most part that it was no more simple country lore and novelists' offcuts than Elgar's music was sentimental pomp and circumstance. It was the critics rather than Hardy's fellow poets who decided he was not a major figure. Even some of the most iconoclastic Modernists held a soft spot for him. Ezra Pound considered Hardy to have given one of only five useful criticisms he had ever received, and he wanted the old man to be sent a copy of his early Cantos. In other cases it was simply that his poetry was not read or (rather like Robert Frost's) assumed to be something it really was not. Beyond a few sneering remarks in *After Strange Gods*, Eliot hardly mentions him, preferring to establish his own full Anglicisation by adopting Kipling. For Yeats, Hardy was an awkward figure, not least because of the resentment amongst Georgians that the obvious Englishman had not yet been awarded the Nobel Prize; and he was only represented by four slight poems in Yeats' *Oxford Book of Modern Verse*, with not one from the *Poems of 1912–13*. Philip Larkin would put that right in 1973 by including twenty-seven in his own Oxford anthology, by far the largest selection in the book (Yeats himself has nineteen, Eliot nine – albeit including the whole of *The Waste Land* and *Little Gidding*), although only one from the sequence we are considering. The point has been made that no selection of Hardy can do him justice, that the various editions that have appeared since he went out of copyright in 1979 are all entirely different books, sometimes sharing no poems at all in common. Most, however, find room for the complete *Poems of 1912–13*.

It is not often that a lyric poet's greatest work is written when he is in his early seventies, but there is a good case for calling this sequence Hardy's masterpiece in verse. He himself would have wished that accolade to go to his epic of the Napoleonic wars, *The Dynasts*, an extraordinary and largely unreadable book, which reveals Hardy's lack of experience in using blank verse as well as his basic theatrical incompetence (this is the man who thought

3

Shakespeare would not be remembered as a playwright). *Poems of 1912–13* demonstrates all Hardy's strengths as a poet alongside those impulses which made him interested in drama, together with the structural sophistication and psychological insight we look for in a novelist.

2

The Marriage

Tom Hardy first met Emma Gifford in March 1870, when he was a church architect on a mission to a remote Cornish coastal parish. He arrived at St Juliot after a tortuous journey; in his pocket was a piece of blue paper, which Emma thought might be church restoration plans, but proved to be some of his poetry. Emma was a very literary person: the idea of a live poet at the rectory, where she lived with her sister and clergyman brother-in-law, and where all she could do was play the piano, paint or go riding, must have thrilled her. Their first encounter in the rectory (still there today, the same porch, the same monkey puzzle he must have walked past) would become part of the poet's personal mythology and much of it reappears in *A Pair of Blue Eyes*. As for Emma, she already felt she knew him, as if she had seen him in a dream.

Emma was almost thirty (like Tom), and had come from Plymouth where she was accustomed to a somewhat genteel life. Her alcoholic father only met her future husband once and evidently disapproved. But then, Tom's mother disapproved of Emma. There was a considerable class difference – although it is interesting that both fathers played the violin. Her family had fallen on hard times and Emma found herself in Cornwall where (as nowadays) one could live relatively cheaply. Tom's arrival on the scene was a great opportunity for her, but stories about her feigning a pregnancy to lure him are surely exaggerations. He was by no means inexperienced with women and one must remember that our picture of Emma is continually distorted by the second Mrs Hardy's accounts. What is certain is that they fell in love, spent much time together, visiting Tintagel (where they got locked in) and the Valency Valley, reading poetry to each other, sharing many incidents which recur in poems outside the sequence we shall be considering and composed at different points in Hardy's long writing career: most famously, 'Under the Waterfall', but also 'Ditty', 'Green Slates', 'At the Word "Farewell"' and 'When I Set Out for Lyonnesse'; it has even been suggested that they have a walk-on part in 'In Time of "the Breaking of Nations"'.

There is no doubt that Emma involved herself in the writing of Hardy's early novels: copying out (most of *Desperate Remedies*), discussing, making alterations (particularly in *Under the Greenwood Tree*). While she could not replace his literary friend Horace Moule, who killed himself some months before their marriage, theirs was a very bookish love affair. Hardy worked on *Far from the Madding Crowd* as he contemplated marriage, jotting ideas down on fragments of leaf and slate as he courted; but significantly he began to keep things from her (such as the title) even at this stage, and there were already tensions between her expectations and those of his new influential friends, including Virginia Woolf's father, Leslie Stephen. Other women were always in the offing, too: the illustrator of *Far from the Madding Crowd*, for one (see 'The Opportunity'). Further poems relevant to this period include 'The Minute before Meeting', 'Love the Monopolist', 'Near Lanivet, 1872' (very prescient), 'I Rose and Went to Rou'tor Town', 'The Chosen', 'Before My Friend Arrived'.

Their marriage took place on 17th September 1874 in Paddington. There has been much speculation about some evident lack of satisfaction during the honeymoon, and the paucity of references to Tom in Emma's diary. Emma would have found her new role difficult, I suspect, more because of servant matters than sexual ones. Yet they were happy in Sturminster Newton, near the Dorset dialect poet William Barnes (whose school pupil Tom had once been), for a year and a half. Here Hardy wrote *The Hand of Ethelberta*, which was badly reviewed, and one of his masterpieces, *The Return of the Native* while Emma was working on her own short stories. Poetry was always to be found ('Honeymoon Time at the Inn', 'We Sat at the Window', 'A Two Years' Idyll', 'Overlooking the River Stour', 'The Musical Box', 'On Sturminster Foot-Bridge', 'The Change' – all these deal with this period) but Hardy knew that only novels would pay the bills.

Emma and Tom now moved to London, finding themselves in Tooting, in a very cold house; he pined for his native Dorset. But they were close to the home of Alexander Macmillan, the publisher, where there were to be many literary soirées and meetings with such figures as Matthew Arnold and Lord Tennyson. Emma was enjoying the high life, but also beginning to find out more about her husband's low-life tendencies and past attachments (particularly his cousin Tryphena Sparks, subject of several poems). Nevertheless, when he fell ill during the writing of *A Laodicean,* she was a constant support and amanuensis. Quarrels there may have been, but many lighter moments too. Poems about this period include 'Beyond the Last Lamp', 'Near Tooting Common', 'A January Night', 'She Charged Me' and 'A Wasted Illness'.

Wimborne Minster was their next home, where Tom wrote *Two on a Tower*, inspired perhaps by the arrival of a comet in June 1881, but they would soon settle for good in Dorchester. The feeling is that Emma did not want to be so much in the pocket of her in-laws ("people of humble origin"), and some critics have speculated that *The Mayor of Casterbridge*, composed at this time, is subliminally about Hardy (like Henchard) 'selling' his wife by making her come to Dorset. The couple's failure to produce a child was unquestionably beginning to tell, Emma becoming rather more intensely religious (having been originally an agnostic), keeping her 'black diaries' and eventually writing a (destroyed) denunciation of Tom in 'What I Think of My Husband'. But on the other hand, certain things still united them: laughter, evidently – a dry wit that Florence, his second wife, would never quite grasp; trips abroad; theatre; church-going (surprisingly in Tom's case); cycling – they both learnt in 1896; women's emancipation; and animal welfare. They kept four cats (one called Kiddley-winkem-poops-Trot!) and a Labrador. The notorious Wessex, who would terrorise the neighbourhood, would only arrive with the second Mrs Hardy. Tom and Emma's shared love of animals was something that never waned. And it must not be forgotten when we dismiss Hardy's first marriage as a failure that the two of them shared a bed for a quarter of a century. Meanwhile, international stardom was calling the novelist – particularly from America, where his popularity was considerable. He, after all, had produced *his* 'children'.

Max Gate, built to Hardy's own design on the outskirts of Dorchester, would be their home from 1885 to their deaths, and it is one of the sets for the drama of *Poems of 1912–13*. Other poems relating to this time are 'He Abjures Love', 'Everything Comes', 'The Conformers', 'I Look Into My Glass', 'Alike and Unlike', 'The Thing Unplanned'. Indeed, he is beginning now to long for the opportunity just to write poetry, and the misunderstandings in reviews of his novels only exacerbate this. Emma was feeling more and more excluded from his creative work, and dissatisfied with her own literary impotency, although a good deal of *The Woodlanders* is in her hand and she contributed in many ways to *Tess of the d'Urbervilles* – there is probably more of her in Tess than anyone else. The latter novel was a huge, if controversial, hit: dinner-party seating plans (says Claire Tomalin) had to be rejigged to take account of the guests' stance on the novel.

It was not until 1899 that the iron entered Emma's soul and she took herself off to an attic room to sleep. She was isolated, feeling that journalists ignored her, visitors mocked her (as indeed many did). She was angry at poems "written to please others – but not me!" She hated Tom's public undermining of religion (she gave him a bible for his fifty-ninth birthday). She was furious that he refused a knighthood. She was occasionally hysterical. She displayed what may have been the beginnings of Alzheimer's. She was not, however, mad, despite Florence Hardy's best efforts to make her appear so. Yes, she had become more narrow-minded and bigoted, offering extreme optimism (in her own book of prose-poems, *Spaces*) to counter Tom's pessimism. But by then, her husband had been dallying with various women (he "needed a muse", writes Tomalin; "they are 'the poison', I am 'the antidote'" wrote Emma), notably Florence Henniker, Agnes Grove and eventually Florence Dugdale, whom Emma would in all innocence invite to be a secretary-companion when she and Tom were having their affair. Hardy himself said of his first wife that "she was peculiar, difficult in some things, but in others she was so simple and childlike". This is something he plays on in the *Poems of 1912–13*, and if anyone is portrayed as crazy it is Thomas Hardy himself (see 'The Phantom Horsewoman'). Other perspectives emerge in poems relevant to these tense years: 'A Broken Appointment', 'Had You Wept', 'At an Inn', 'The Division', 'A Thunderstorm in Town', 'The Month's Calendar', 'In Death Divided', 'The Interloper', 'Wives in the Sere', 'In Tenebris', 'God's Funeral', 'After the Visit', 'A Second Attempt', 'Between Us Now'. *Wessex Poems,* which would appear in 1898, was rumoured to have caused Emma "more pain perhaps than any other single work" (Seymour-Smith). But it was probably *Jude the Obscure* that began the pain. She was not alone. Hardy received hate-mail, including the ashes of the book, and it convinced him that he must now focus on his first love: not Emma, but poetry.

Much of his poetic energy went into that grand dramatic folly, *The Dynasts* (conceived alongside that altogether slighter Napoleonic prose work, *The Trumpet-Major*); it would eventually be received with a mixture of bemusement and acclaim. His lyric poetry, however, was continually snubbed. As Emma's final months approached (and the events and feelings of the time are captured in various poems: 'The Sight', 'Something Tapped', 'When Oats Were Reaped'), there were low points such as a fierce quarrel on Christmas Day, 1910 and highlights such as a garden party on 16th July 1912, or the day that autumn when she took out all her old sheet music and played through her old songs on the piano (see 'The Last Performance'), before announcing that she would never play again. But she was clearly declining, needing a regular sedative of sherry, pure alcohol and opium.

On 22nd November, Emma visited a friend six miles off and suffered 'indigestion' in the night; on the 25th, she was feeling unwell when some other rather insensitive friends imposed themselves on her even though she was clearly sick. The next day she saw the doctor, "who did not think her seriously ill" (Florence Hardy's *Life*) and Tom felt he could happily go to the rehearsal for a local production of *The Trumpet-Major*, not knowing that his wife's death (probably from impacted gallstones) was imminent and would in fact be announced from the stage at the première. The audience would include many of the significant people in the Hardys' life together. When he returned to Max Gate from the rehearsal, she was in bed and he did not go up to see her; next morning she deteriorated and died. "Emma's death was absolutely unexpected by me, the doctor, & everybody, though not sudden, strictly speaking. She was quite well a week before ...", wrote Hardy, adding: "I was with her when she passed away." Then began the grief, the remembering, the haunting, the lacerating self-reproach which would shortly find its way into *Poems of 1912–13*.

3

Poems of 1912–13

In *The Modern Poetic Sequence* (OUP, 1986), M.L. Rosenthal and Sally M. Gall claim *Poems of 1912–13* to be "the first developed English sequence", anticipating Yeats' civil war poems by a decade, and cultivating a taste for the kind of thing that would be regarded as 'modern' (though Hardy clings still to an 'old-fashioned' narrative). They are putting the eminent Victorian into a context that includes Pound, Williams, Stevens, Auden, Lowell; but there is no doubt that Hardy's approach to grief is still an inspiration to verse elegists (Douglas Dunn, Penelope Shuttle, Thom Gunn, Elaine Feinstein ...). Rosenthal and Gall make the astute point that criticism of the sequence "tends to single out certain poems for discussion and ignore its character as a moving structure ... its powerful push towards self-discovery against the terrible odds" – that self-discovery being "the recovery of one's most generously empathic possibilities". They remind us too that Hardy originally intended only eighteen of the poems to appear, ending with 'The Phantom Horsewoman'. In fact, he wrote at least fifty poems in memory of Emma during this time.

The final arrangement, however, is almost symphonic: a 'first movement' of seven poems establishing the emotional and physical territory, the facts of the rocky marriage, the sudden loss; a 'second movement' consisting of five poems during which Emma is given a right of reply (trying to make Tom understand how she felt about their life) and prepares us for his actual, if futile, return to her Cornwall; a richly complex Largo 'third movement' of another five substantial poems, chiefly set on the Cornish coast, in which (as Rosenthal and Gall put it) "the search occurs and succeeds", but in which "the landscape remains unheeding"; then a final movement, where there is a change of perspective (and narrator) and a gradual disappearance of the wife's spirit, concluding with a return to the Dorset (not the Cornish) coast "where the picnic was".

The motto Hardy places at the head of his sequence is *Veteris vestigia flammae*, which comes from the fourth Book of Virgil's *Aeneid* and can be translated as "relics of the old fire" or perhaps "traces of an old flame". Robert Fitzgerald's version runs: "I recognise/The signs of the old flame, of old desire ..." The line is, significantly, from Queen Dido's speech of self-justification about her new love: "Had I not set my face against remarriage/After my first love died ...?" The use of a motto also reminds us that (as Hardy's other 'ghost' has him say in her ghost-written *Life*): "the business of the poet and novelist is to show the sorriness underlying the grandest things, and the grandeur underlying the sorriest things." Many thought Emma Hardy a sorry thing; others have suggested that Thomas Hardy wanted to be considered something grand, which is why he reminds us that he knows his Virgil.

Hardy was reticent about publishing the Emma poems ("Some of them I rather shrink from printing") but decided he would do so "as the only amends I can make" (letter to Florence Henniker). When the new collection did appear, in November 1914, the world was more concerned with the Western Front than *Satires of Circumstance*. There was little positive reaction to the collection as a whole and the sequence itself was generally ignored. Lytton Strachey was one of the few who saw through the apparent clumsiness and felt something "touching our marrow-bones". Mrs Hardy II, however, took offence at the work, seeming to misunderstand what her husband was doing. *Poems of 1912–13* commemorates the end of more than one marriage.

I The Going

The sequence of twenty-one poems opens with a title whose definite article and gerund might be a gentle homage to the Metaphysicals, who were masters of the elegy. By December 1912, when 'The Going' was composed, Hardy (since the 1890s no longer a novelist) was increasingly conscious of the tradition to which he had abandoned himself – that of Henry King's 'Exequy' for his late wife as well as Donne's raunchier love poems. We are inclined to think that interest in these poets only revived with Eliot, but there is much of their manner in Hardy, not least in the taste for elaborate verse forms, although he reserves the right to the kind of freedom that he regarded as the sign of good poetry. "The whole secret of a living style", he wrote in Florence Hardy's *Life,* "lies in not having too much style – being, in fact, a little careless, or rather seeming to be, here and there." He goes on to quote Herrick's "sweet disorder in the dress ..."

'The Going' employs six seven-line stanzas, whose rhyme-pattern and line-lengths alternate to match the poem's structure: "Why did you ...?", "Never to ...", "Why do you ...?" "You were she ...", "Why, then ...?", "Well, well!". For those who dismiss Hardy the poet as a rather metronomic craftsman, it is worth noting that he is not rigidly counting syllables here, but he *is* listening to beats and using something which Hopkins – who died just before Hardy gave up the novel – would have called "sprung rhythm". In fact it is just the sense of word and pulse that anyone used to singing a folk-song will recognise: "Why did you give no hint that night", with its perfect eight-syllable tetrameter carries the same four beats as "You would close your term here, up and be gone", despite its ten syllables, or "At the end of the alley of bending boughs" with its eleven. He subtly shifts from the feminine-rhyming couplet rhythm of "Where I could not follow/With wing of swallow", which is fixed in the fifth and sixth lines of every variation, to the more assertive trimeters which open the second, fourth and final stanzas, with their stressed initial words ("Never ..." "You ..." "Well ...").

It hardly needs to be said what a moving poem this is: the horrible repositioning of every recent shared event in the light of Emma's death; the aching need to say a last farewell; time and nature's stony indifference; the hallucinations that accompany grief; the sickening realisation and the inevitable recourse to something more living and "red-veined" – the passionate memories they shared from their days in Cornwall. And naturally the poem is made all the more touching to our divorce-ridden times by the revelation that the couple "did not speak" – or at least (depending on how we read the line-breaks) "did not speak ... of those days". But I think we do need reminding what a virtuoso performance Hardy puts on and the many musical felicities in 'The Going': the tiny echo of "if" in "indifferent" and "those" in "abode", the suitably tensile leap in the colloquialism "up and be gone", the gentle alliteration of "wish for a word, while I" lulling us before the shock of "saw morning harden upon the wall"; or the sinuous syntax, clauses playing between the rhymes and weaving their way like sheep under the eye of Gabriel Oak's old dog. Each of the first four stanzas is a single sentence: only in the penultimate one does Hardy change this, after "time's renewal". The final stanza, however, consists of five sentences, the last two fragmented by the pressure of emotion as the poet confesses that he seems "but a dead man held on end/To sink down soon", an image partly of the gallows (one of Hardy's preoccupations), partly of drowning, and partly of being dangled like bait on a line. In any case, that verb 'undo' has all kinds of resonance: from the knot of marriage to the noose of the hanged man.

II Your Last Drive

Despite her numerous infirmities (breathlessness, difficulty in walking and, according to Martin Seymour-Smith, "brief bouts of dementia") Emma was remarkably energetic to the end, even taking to her bike once or twice. Cycling had been one of their shared pleasures. But the first Mrs Hardy's "last drive" was just that: "she motored to pay a visit six

14

miles off", the second wife's *Life* informs us, on the afternoon of a damp, dark 22nd November, two days before her seventy-second birthday. The road, of course, was a "moorway", not a "motorway" as the modern eye tends to misread the opening line: "Here by the moorway you returned,/And saw the borough [Dorchester] lights ahead/ That lit your face ..." But even if it were, the sentiment would be equally effective, framed by the poet's customary enjambments, guiding the sentence through his contraflow to the stanza end as in 'The Going'.

The omniscient narrator imagines what he did not see. As he will explain in 'The Walk', they did not think of each other as "left behind", although naturally Hardy does not mention that his mind now was on other women entirely. There is a good deal of guilt, of "protesting too much" in the third stanza: even if he *had* been there, he wouldn't have noticed any "last-time look in the flickering sheen". That is merely the kind of poeticism the experienced writer recreates, he suggests, and reinforces the point by mentioning "the writing upon your face". He recalls Emma commenting on "the charm of that haloed view/That never again would beam on you". The beatification of the landscape (and implicitly of the wife's memory) is begun with touches worthy of Renaissance masters, who knew how to use religious highlights for the worldliest of ends: "lights ... lit ... haloed ... beam ...". The very place where Emma was to be buried – Stinsford churchyard, 'Mellstock' – was on her route, something Hardy cannot be expected to overlook. "Eight days later": he tolls the irony with three 'a'-sounding strokes, echoing them with an alliterative "lie" at the end of the line, itself to be picked up by the "heedless eye", which rhymes so casually, so painfully two lines on. Whether the awkwardness of "be spoken of as one who was not" conveys the discomfort and unease, or whether there were better alternatives, the reader can decide. The repeated monosyllables are something the poet would not have wanted to lose.

There are private hints and shadows in this poem, as in any good love poem. The churchyard would have seemed "alien" to Emma, because she did not expect to die just yet; but it had long been "alien" to this Cornish girl. Her spirit would be out on Beeny Cliff or at least in a different, more exposed church – St Juliot (locally pronounced 'jilt' – which must have amused Hardy). But Emma, like any Hardy heroine, is allowed to speak her mind, and we hear the voice of a real character – abrupt, unsentimental, independent – in the six lines of the fourth stanza. Do what you like, you old fool: I'm not here to interfere any more. Hardy knows already what he has put her through and he is not going to let himself off the hook. He does allow himself a humble – not to say cowed – reply, however: a contrite sigh, a couple of rhetorical questions (Am I going to criticize you now? Did I ever not do things because people didn't care?) and a resigned conclusion, using the rhythms of the Prayer Book in the final litany: "past love, praise, indifference, blame".

III The Walk

In *Poems of 1912–13* Hardy sets lighter movements alongside more extended adagios, the effect being somewhat like a musical suite. 'The Walk' is a mere sixteen lines: two identically shaped stanzas, whose momentum comes from the full rhyme and persistent walking rhythms. It is only when we read poets of the period who try to use rhyme with a similar unabashed confidence (Georgian best-seller Wilfrid Gibson for one) that we begin to appreciate what an achievement it is to make a lyric like this sound natural. Notice for instance how the rhyme in lines 13 and 14 requires us to pronounce "again" as "agen", rather than the more formally enunciated alternative. The whole poem sounds perfectly uncontrived, with little observed details ("gated ways"; the "hilltop tree" – probably Culliford Tree) and a feeling that the poet is not being bullied into taking a certain direction. In 'The Walk', in fact, every rhyme word is essential, everything (pauses included) is designed to culminate in the psychological and emotional insight at the end of each stanza: firstly, that he "did not mind,/Not thinking of you as left behind"; secondly, that now she is for ever left behind, retracing his old steps and returning home can no longer be a casual matter. Her absence pervades the 'look' of the room – or "*a* room", which is a telling distinction as it suggests that Hardy cannot quite bring himself to specify, he has to look away, and in any case their shared living space might now just as well be anywhere. This final couplet – its long, pondering, painful realisation – is a moving surprise, touchingly understated, an answer to an idle question: "What difference, then?" Wordsworth's Lucy is somewhere here ("But she is in her Grave, and Oh,/The difference to me"), a reminder that Hardy is not so distraught that he can resist a literary echo. "Returning thence" might not be quite how Wordsworth would have chosen to end a poem, but the rhyme word certainly links the writer's arrival back home with the consciousness of Emma's absence, reminding us now that she has no "sense" (the final rhyme), that she "is – elsewhere".

IV Rain on a Grave

Hardy's various biographers all have their theories about the precise source of dissent between Emma and Tom, but no one denies there was a breach. The *Poems of 1912–13* represent an attempt to mend that breach, even though by this time it was as wide as eternity itself. In 'Rain on a Grave' (in manuscript 'Rain on Her Grave'), the poet is perhaps overcompensating by briefly wishing that they could be buried together. Hardy seems to have forgotten his own "workhouse irony", the poem 'A Curate's Kindness', where the "young Pa'son" thinks to ease the suffering of a married couple who would normally be sent to different institutions. He decides "they shall abide them/In one wing together" and the narrator's face falls: "To get freed of her there was the one thing/Had made the change welcome to me". In fact, both of Hardy's wives would be buried at Stinsford with him – or with his heart, once it was salvaged from the biscuit tin where a surgeon had placed it (unless indeed, as the tale runs, a cat got it first!). The heartless remains of Thomas Hardy were interred in Westminster

Abbey.

J.O. Bailey points out that Hardy's poems commonly move from "a pleasant illusion to a realization of fact", but that this begins with dismay and ends in serenity. The image of water despoiling a grave inevitably brings to mind the undoing of Troy's attempts to put right the wrongs he did to Fanny Robin in *Far from the Madding Crowd*. In both cases, there is a sense of a malevolent power at work. Hardy does not develop the self-flagellating aspect of the scene in his poem, but its forcefulness is clear enough from the hollow-sounding opening words ("Clouds spout"). The entire poem makes use of this heavy spondee rhythm ("Her who ... One who ... We both ... Green blades"), an unnerving *drip-drop* that runs down all four stanzas. Hardy is chiefly interested in the ironic fact that his wife had always hated the indignity of getting wet in a rainstorm. He seems to smile at this memory, although one can imagine it was an irritation in life ("birds close their bills" may imply that he knew when to keep quiet) and there is no doubt something Freudian in Emma's reaction, as well as in those words "coldly", "disdain", "shivered". 'Rain on a Grave' is, however, a touching portrait of the dead woman: we can visualise exactly the movements Hardy describes in the second stanza and the outburst in the opening lines of the third is fully earned: we have already been shown nature in tears.

The thought that the two of them should be buried together is not dwelt on for long: the poet realises almost as soon as he says it that he's better off keeping his thoughts above ground: " – who would stray there/When sunny the day there,/Or evening was clear/At the prime of the year". Stinsford, as we have already seen, was a favourite place of theirs to walk to. But what Hardy does now is something familiar from poems such as 'Voices from Things Growing in a Churchyard', where he imagines intercourse between nature and the dead, the processes of decay transmuting the essence of an individual into some appropriate tree or flower. In Emma's case (had he been reading her *Some Recollections*?), it is the coming daisies that catch the poet's imagination, snatching an image ("like stars on the ground") which echoes Romeo's balcony speech. Soon, he says, she will "form part of them – /Ay – the sweet heart of them" (playing affectionately on 'sweetheart'), and he ends the poem by using the daisies – which, it is to be noted, have not yet actually appeared – to highlight Emma's simple goodness, the "child's pleasure" she once took in these particular flowers. Fanny Robin is not so very far away.

V I Found Her Out There

The fifth of the poems is one of the most elemental: the "loamy cell" in which Emma rests is far from the "western sea" and its "blind gales" (a nice image for the uncaring power of that particular element and a reminder of the way a cliff-top wind can actually force one's eyelids closed). The fourth element is in the thought of Emma gazing from St Juliot "At Dundagel's [Tintagel's] famed head,/While the dipping blaze/Dyed her face fire-red". Not the most flattering portrait, with a touch of the reddleman (not to say hellfire) about it. Nevertheless, 'I Found Her Out There' pulses with affectionate energy, particularly in the play between iambic and anapaestic metres at the start of lines, the former used to suggest solidity in the first line of the opening stanza – a solidity which is undermined as the metre falls away in a cluster of stressed words in line two and only just clings on in three: "I *found* her out there/On a *slope few see*/That *falls westwardly* ..." Terra firma is only regained (after a final metrical shaking by the hurricane) in the stanza's last, perfectly iambic line.

The passionate content of the poem is heard as it were through a sea-shell, distantly, almost hollowly: it feels far off, as it is, as it should be, since that was in the past in Cornwall and "here" is now in Dorset: "a noiseless nest/No sea beats near". That sea is as symbolic as in any Hardy novel, but it is worth remembering as we read the word "nest" that Emma and Hardy were childless, something which blighted their marriage. The high winds of family life are something that never shook Max Gate. Perhaps it is those unborn children (rather than Merlin or Uther Pendragon) that are on "those haunted heights". Hardy imagines his future wife sighing "at the tale/Of sunk Lyonnesse", Cornwall's version of the Atlantis legend, but associated popularly with the great lover Tristan – particularly so in the mind of Thomas Hardy, because of his affection for Algernon Swinburne. *Tristram of Lyonnesse* (1882) may be forgotten today, but Hardy would certainly have known it. The fact that "a wind-tugged tress/Flapped her cheek like a flail" surely cannot be a wicked allusion to Swinburne's fascination with sado-masochism, but it is a curious simile, suggesting at best a cruel fate ready to thresh the love out of Emma's life before it has even properly ripened. The "murmuring miles" are the kind of word-music Victorian poets such as Swinburne and Tennyson specialised in. The poem's conclusion, however, is pure Hardy: the ghost of Emma, like a character from a stage melodrama, somehow creeping underground (old tin mines? or are ghosts unhampered by such problems?) to her old home. That word "domiciled" is not only convenient for the rhyme with "child" (ironically, Hardy likes to think of her in that way) but also reminds us of his own earliest poem, 'Domicilium', some of whose themes are touched on here. So the two one-time lovers were united from the start, "all unknowing", each in their west-facing homes, each on "uncultivated slopes" and "quite alone".

VI Without Ceremony

If Emma was in the last poem a treasure that Hardy "found" out in the wilds of North Cornwall, here she is one that has slipped unnoticed from his hand. 'Without Ceremony' is the least ceremonious of elegies, with its informal opening, its familiar register: nothing of the grand symphonic Hardy here; this is chamber music. One can see the appeal Hardy held for British composers such as Benjamin Britten and notably Gerald Finzi, who set several of the *Poems of 1912–13:* the words invite accompaniment, but are not impossibly assertive. 'Without Ceremony''s rhyme-scheme is different again (*abccb*), although the enjambments at certain bustling moments are characteristic of what one might call Hardy's own 'swift style': "I hastened in/To rejoin you" … "a mind to career/Off anywhere" … "disappear/For ever" …

The poem is spun around Hardy's recollection of the fact that his wife was essentially an independent creature. Even though he speaks gently of her ("It was your way, my dear …"), the reader can only deduce that all was not well between them if she really behaved like this. In the tradition of fierce-spirited Hardy heroines, Emma could be forthright and unsentimental, despite the childlike quality noted elsewhere. It must not be forgotten just how much Emma had been involved in the writing of her husband's earlier novels: she was a good deal more than a simple Wessex maid and there was plenty going on behind "her childlike face" (Claire Tomalin). Recent biographers such as Tomalin and before her, Martin Seymour-Smith, have tried to piece together how the Hardys' marriage worked, her reactions to his roving eye, his to her puritanism and increasing eccentricity. Outsiders seem to have had conflicting reactions towards Emma, the harshest being Mrs R.L. Stevenson's: "*very* plain, quite underbred, and most tedious". What occurs to the poet himself – who remarked elsewhere of Emma that "she was so *living*" – is that she died as she had often acted in life: unceremoniously, without notice (something disputed by Robert Gittings, but generally agreed on now). Does Hardy himself lurch towards the sentimental at moments like this? Not here, I think, although there are dangerous tendencies elsewhere in the sequence. We admire these fifteen lines for the unaffected honesty, the subtle deployment of rhyme, the quiet insight into a revealing aspect of Tom and Emma's domestic life.

VII Lament

Here is another poem beginning with a poignant flash of memory, a sudden consciousness of absence. Hardy realises that the weather is the kind which would have moved Emma to invite guests: he describes a "bright-hatted and gloved"

Victorian garden party full of light and smiles, an occasion made possible (or does the metaphor suggest it was never possible?) by "friendship's spell" – not quite what we associate with drab Max Gate. But Hardy defined Art as "the secret of how to produce by a false thing the effect of a true" (*Life*) and he admired those artists (such as Turner) who could manipulate light into "landscape *plus* a man's soul". 'Lament''s opening scene is painted with the luminosity of a dream. In reality, the Hardys were frequently imposed on: the account of how the imperious Owen sisters barged in, dragged the sick Emma downstairs and demanded that she fetch her husband (he was writing, not wishing to be disturbed) is one of the more piteous anecdotes from her last days. Interestingly, she managed to hold them off until Rebekah Owen herself dispatched Emma's maid to fetch her idol. At any rate, the "spell" of Hardy's imagining unwinds in a series of rhymes: "spell ... shell ... cell" and the lucent dream-vision dissipates.

But in the second stanza another comes in its place: a dinner party, with Emma genuinely delighting in the role of hostess. The vision goes again – very much in the tradition of Romantic poets and Schubert song-cycles – and "She is shut under grass/Where no cups flow/Powerless to know/That it might be so." That last phrase anticipates 'The Oxen' of 1915, where the closest Hardy can come to religious hope is "Hoping it might be so"; and here, the best he can do to comfort himself is to remind himself of his late wife's own innocence. Not daisies this time, but snowdrops and crocuses. Flowers, of course, commemorate the dead, but they also go on reappearing long after the dead are forgotten, "Wholly possessed/By an infinite rest". The latter lines are unsettling: "possessed" suggests death's greed and ruthlessness, its unmitigated evil; "infinite" puts paid to any hope and not even the comforting sound of "rest" can help.

The conclusion of 'Lament' is in the tone of one "possessed" by the staleness of the living world (notice how "stale" picks up on the sound of "staying"). No party or dinner or even display of flowers can bring any comfort to the grieving partner, any more than it can for dead Emma. The bitterness dribbles from "junketings" to alliterative "joy her" to rhyming "cloy her" in the same downward spiral of despair. Hardy the church architect notes "her yew-arched bed", as if to imply the futility of all he has done since he met her at St Juliot, even of the Victorian age itself, with its own many proud arches; and perhaps it is not suggesting too much to hear "you" whispering in "yew"?

VIII The Haunter

It is hard to read *Poems of 1912–13* and not wonder about Florence Dugdale, who became the second Mrs Hardy in February 1914. Martin Seymour-Smith sees the marriage as bad news and it certainly was for Emma's reputation: Florence played up the suggestion that her predecessor was mad. She herself longed to be commemorated in verse, as Emma had been repeatedly, sometimes slyly, sometimes cruelly, although more often "to touch our hearts by showing his own" (Leslie Stephen): indeed, Tom's poetry was very much at the heart of his relationship with Emma – and the outside world never quite appreciated the value of either. 'After the Visit' is definitely about Florence. 'The Sigh' might be about Florence (Seymour-Smith thinks so); and 'To Meet, or Otherwise' sounds as though it describes their affair. There are other lyrics too in which a possible mistress is encoded with the kind of ingenuity Eastern European poets would later use to keep their feelings from the secret police. But for every one such there are half a dozen patently about Emma. 'The Haunter' suggests that she remains the one true companion and in a letter to Rider Haggard from 1913, Hardy explained how "loss becomes more apparent and grievous" the more time passes.

Hardy was writing when Spiritualism was extremely popular (the First World War would make it even more so). Its rituals of séance and ouija held the kind of bleak fascination reserved in our day for reality TV. The ghosts in many of Hardy's poems are occasionally cartoon affairs, melodramatic or comic devices, but during these pre-war years he read a good deal of M.R. James, whose ghostly narratives convey a chilling authenticity. He also began seeing things himself (he had always longed to): in Stinsford churchyard, laying holly on his grandfather's grave, the 18th-century gentleman himself appeared, made an enigmatic remark about a "green Christmas" and vanished into the church; then in his final year he told Florence how he had observed "a dark man" beside her at a tea party. In the Emma lyrics there is at least the suggestion of his willingness to acknowledge that there are more things in heaven and earth. Even if it did not quite happen to him (his dog Wessex seems to have had the gift), Hardy would be familiar enough with the commonplace experience of 'seeing' a relative at the time of their death. He leaves the door open a crack and the result is rather more than *Blithe Spirit* and a good deal less than Yeats' *A Vision*, but in taking Emma seriously he was having also to take her religious beliefs seriously and reassess his own.

'The Haunter' is the first poem in the sequence to employ dramatic monologue, thus taking the author deeper still into his subject's personality. The 'ghost' knows how those habits that used to irritate (her hovering near by when he was trying to work!) are the very things he now misses; but she laments that she cannot "answer the words he lifts me" – an astute choice of verb and not one forced on the poet by the rather discreet rhyme-scheme. It suggests an offering – to a Muse, or at least for approval. Ironically, Hardy has chosen to use Emma's own imagined words to comment on how his preoccupation with writing separates them (although it once united them): "Never he sees my faithful phantom/Though he speaks thereto." What he "speaks" are her very words, the reply she says she cannot give. She describes accompanying his "fancy" to the places that have become Emma, most touchingly evoked in "Where the shy hares print long paces,/Where the night rooks go", details which tell us of her own strange reticence (hares are creatures rich in occult mythology) and hint at a lost sexuality from Lyonnesse. St Juliot comes to mind as the poem leads us "Into old aisles where the past is all to him ..."

At the end of 'The Haunter', Hardy tries to capture Emma's childlike manner this time in her actual speaking voice ("What a good haunter I am ...") – his way of reminding us that he knows the words he is writing are part of a game, that the 'ghost' is merely a psychic manifestation of "all that love can do"; and yet by the time the page is printed, Emma is at least as real as Ted Hughes' 'Thought Fox'.

IX The Voice

Even when we come to such a well-known individual lyric, we should be thinking of these poems as a sequence. After all, we have just been listening to 'the voice' of Emma in 'The Haunter'. This is the survivor's side of the story: he hears her call, but the words he thinks he can make out are very different from those in the previous poem. This spirit is trying to tell him that she is no longer the woman of their latter years – eccentric, suspicious, religiose, time-torn Mrs Hardy – but has become lovely young Emma Gifford again, even wearing the same blue dress (how significant that colour blue was for them). The poet is only briefly persuaded: he doubts it almost as soon as he thinks he has heard it, needing to "view" her, to convince the rationalist, the sceptic in him. The voice, Hardy seems to have decided by the third stanza, was a trick of the wind: he collapses back into his grief, taking the poem's metre with him. And yet the last line has 'the woman calling'.

'The Voice' is justly celebrated, from the first line's kissing 'm's and inverted word order (so that "Woman" begins the poem) to its brilliant expression of despair in the final stanza. The dominant waltzing dactylic metre exactly matches the hypnagogic mood of the opening, but what seems at a first reading a conventional cry from the heart over a lost love proves far more complex, psychologically and grammatically. The one-sentence first stanza manages to encapsulate the story of Tom and Emma's relationship, rhymes highlighting key elements ("were" ... "fair" – one has to adopt an Edwardian pronunciation for "wair"). There follows a tentative questioning – as much about Hardy's own mental state as about the possibility of life after death. There is a defiant response to his own momentary lapse in common sense ("Can it be you that I hear?") when he counters: "Let me view you, then ...", like Hamlet demanding more and more evidence at Elsinore. It is into the poet's head that we are drawn in this second stanza, where what he wishes begins to merge with what he witnesses. He does not see her in "the original air-blue gown"; he demands to see her in it. The rhythmical magic of that phrase is Hardy at his best, and it comes from a sudden shift in metre to something less clearly defined and from the delicate cluster of syllables in "original" juxtaposed with three softly affirmative stresses: "aír-blúe gówn". The effect is like that of a revelatory moment in a film where the background music suddenly stops playing.

By the time doubt has taken root in the third stanza, the normal dactylic rhythms and triple rhymes of life "in its listlessness" have reasserted themselves. This is indeed "landscape *plus* a man's soul", a landscape evoked as much through sound as picture: the clagginess of "wet mead", the sibilant chill of "listlessness", and the dead winter crust on "wan wistlessness" – the latter word a source of considerable discomfort among critics of Hardy, but they perhaps did not feel with what appropriate sluggishness it falls from the tongue.

As I have already suggested, the poem's triumph is the coda, Beethovenian in its unexpectedness. The lilting dream waltz has gone and with it the last vestiges of optimism. The language is charged with drama, economical and potent in a way Hardy seldom was in his actual stage writing: "Thus I" drops disconsolately, followed by the caesura, then a broken shuffle of a phrase: "faltering forward". The poet is deluded, is hearing things, is a foolish fond old man obsessed with the past ("leaves around me falling"). But for all those heartfelt leaves that he has let fall from his desk, he expresses his despair in a music more enduring than

Swinburne's and the equal of Tennyson's: "Wind oozing thin through the thorn from norward". This blend of '*oo*', '*I*', '*or*' and '*th*' sounds is a spectacular piece of euphony: its impassioned length makes the following six-syllable whimper "And the woman calling" all the more piteous.

X His Visitor

Mrs Florence Hardy must have been very irritated by these four stanzas. In 1916, she complained to Rebekah Owen how she "may not alter the shape of a garden bed, or cut down or move the smallest bush, any more than I may alter the position of an article of furniture". Her dead rival sees things rather differently. In 'His Visitor' (continuing the spectral theme), Hardy once again lets his protagonist speak for herself and the voice he gives her is lively, playful, unliterary, reflecting his own continuing interest in the theatre – and actresses! – at this time.

Emma has floated along from Mellstock (that is to say, her burial place at Stinsford) apparently to inspect Max Gate. One is reminded of the placard for the housemaid that she hung in the hall: "When dusting, please *blow* but do not touch." Her presence is made all the more fanciful by the moonlight that accompanies her and by her promise to "go in the gray, at the passing of the mail-train". That sardonic allusion to the material world reminds the reader that life has moved on, that she is merely an old-fashioned poet's fantasy. So too does the fact that she won't need to use a door when she leaves (Hardy's wry sense of humour often baffled Florence, but it was something he shared with his first wife).

The poet's use of a Middle English 'bob' technique – i.e., a short last line – arms each stanza with a potential barb, to which Hardy naturally adds a deadly drop of rhyme. The form's origin ("bob and wheel") is with bell-ringing: a tolling note calls the ghost back to her grave at the poem's end in the deep vowels of "manifold/Souls of old". The "As before" bob might just be a regretful sigh; "Float along" is Hardy being facetious about the ghost's powers of locomotion; but

"As with me" at the end of the second stanza is clearly meant to suggest rivalry (Emma has noticed that her iconic daisies have been cleared, the tea service is different, there has been painting – of the *un*artistic kind – and a general lack of cosiness).

Several details of Emma's personality and interests emerge: her frustrated ambitions as an artist, her delight in singing, her household efficiency ("my rule"), but we are also reminded of her unstable constitution ("feeble hours and strong") and her impulsiveness ("So I don't want to linger ..."). The repetition in the third stanza of "never" emphasises not only that time has moved on, but that soon no one will be left who can tell Emma Gifford's story, say what the girl from St Juliot was really like, bring to life the "pair of blue eyes" in that famously unphotogenic face. As Hardy perhaps suspected, Florence would do her best to excise Emma from the *Life*.

XI A Circular

At the eye of the sequence, 'A Circular' picks up on the material concerns of the previous poem. Tom finds himself reading what Emma perhaps came to prefer to his own writings – a clothes catalogue. To the last she had a taste for what Robert Gittings calls "girlish fashions of a bygone age". There is an unspoken rebuke by her husband here (this is the man who had a parcel of his second wife's purchases sent straight back to the shop), but by making these twelve simple lines the mid-point of *Poems of 1912–13*, Hardy manages to suggest both the hollowness of life without Emma and the transience of the 'up-to-date' fripperies that she so loved. The "vaingloriousness" that he had noted in his "lines on the loss of the *Titanic*" (composed only half a year before her death) recurs here. "Deep from human vanity ... stilly couches she," he wrote of the ship in that intensely sexual masterpiece. Emma would certainly have relished the mirrors, jewels and "gilded gear": she too had been emotionally, spiritually "in a solitude of the sea" with her "far and dissociate" iceberg of a husband.

The advertising 'circular' designed for idle browsing (omen of our own commercialisation – just one of the many changes Thomas Hardy foresaw) is here inspected because he, the widower, is "legal representative". The vulgarity of it all is evident in Hardy's choice of the word "shout" in the ninth line: Emma, by contrast, is silenced; her only clothes are her grave-cloth. If we have been reading the full sequence, we have just seen her ghost take her leave of Hardy's world – no longer concerned about clothes (or doors even), but valuing nevertheless lost familiar comforts. Typically, the rhyme clinches the poem: "proud" leads inevitably round to "shroud": an all too obvious irony, it could be said, but also a gentle observation on the general circularity of things – an idea that recurs, with apt symmetry, in ten poems' time.

XII A Dream or No

"Why go to St Juliot ...?" The *genius loci* still presides in this concluding poem of the second 'movement' (as defined by Rosenthal and Gall). It was composed in February 1913 and Hardy did return to North Cornwall in early March, determined to be there for the anniversary of his original visit on the 7th. But he found the experience "very painful ... I wish I had not come – What possessed me to do it!" These words are quoted in a letter by the future Mrs Hardy II, who adds that she knew it was unwise and expects "he will come back this afternoon, very miserable". Hardy knew what Florence wanted to hear.

'A Dream or No' begins, then, with self-questioning and an admission of how much St Juliot means to him: "much of my life claims the spot as its key." The poet's heart, in other words, will for ever remain in that consecrated Cornish ground, whatever lies in Stinsford – and although, in fact, he and Emma chose to marry in prosaic Paddington. Yet the place itself is to him like something out of a dream, in which Emma becomes the presiding deity of a sacred grove: "Fair-eyed and white-shouldered, broad-browed and brown-tressed", the paired compound adjectives emphasising companionship and coupling. Hardy says, as in the cycle's fifth poem, that he "found her" as if fate had willed it: he could have used 'met', but he likes the notion that (a) it was his initiative and (b) he was under the spell of "some strange necromancy" (he returned to Dorset with "magic" in his eyes according to 'When I Set Out for Lyonnesse'). The "sea-birds around her" symbolise that there was freedom in the air when they met, but remind us too that their relationship was to be (as she herself described it) "erratically minded and *actioned*". Robert Gittings thought that she always liked the idea of their being "two carefree vagabonds, blown by the wind of artistic impulse".

The poem's form suggests the uncertainty: long line/short line (the longer ones generally rooted in 1913, the shorter central couplets harking back to 1870), a shifting metre, beginning trochaically, then moving to something more anapaestic, but never quite settling down. In the third stanza, the Emma is more of an enchantress, less romantic than necromantic, drawing the lover in with cunning enjambments: not quite a succubus, but archetypal in form. Though Freud was alive and influential by now, the poet is at pains to assure us that he was as sceptical about this dream as he had been about the ghosts. Yet as he wonders how it can have been the same girl he was living with at Max Gate up until a few months ago, the metaphor he deploys is revealing: "Can she ever have been here/And shed her life's sheen here ...?" Apart from the appeal of the alliteration, what did Hardy mean by that last phrase? That she left a superficial glamour behind her? That she was consumed by polishing and dusting? Or something more grotesque (as in the *Titanic* poem): a kind of glowing trail? Could he mean that she had bestowed ("shed") a living light on those who knew her? Or is it simply that Hardy thought her most alive in St Juliot (Juliet to his Romeo) and that by marrying him she had changed roles, "shed" that life: the snake casts its skin and loses Eden? It is a richly ambiguous passage.

Hardy is no modernist and cannot leave such uncertainty,

so he is obliged to return us to a Celtic twilight, a misty finale like the shimmering of Arnold Bax's *Tintagel* or the end of Elgar's Second Symphony (completed on that same coast in 1911). The language of the place is nevertheless charged with sexuality: "a Vallency Valley/With stream and leafed alley" speaks for its Freudian self, "Beeny" sounds like a lovers' pet name, "Bos" (shorn of its "-castle") has a distinctly buxom quality, and "its flounce flinging mist" makes it clear that for Hardy – as for Bax and Elgar – this was a feminine landscape. Tom in his seventies had a roving eye, but (as Florence Dugdale was beginning to suspect) it was his original Muse that could stir him above all things.

XIII After a Journey

We are on the coastal path above the lonely, brooding Pentargan Bay, a little further along from Boscastle, on the way to Beeny Cliff. The bay itself is nowadays inaccessible but its physical make-up is obviously deeply symbolic to a mind of Thomas Hardy's cast: a single thread of water falling in front of a concealed dark cave. Anyone who has walked this stretch will know that it is physically demanding. For Hardy it was an emotional struggle too, although he wrote of the satisfaction he found in "putting on the manners of ghosts, wandering in their haunts, and taking their views of surrounding things". He admits in 'After a Journey' that he is moving "frailly"; nevertheless, the sexual energy evident in the previous poem continues to crackle here: the "unseen waters' ejaculations", the girl's "rose-flush coming and going ..." The ghost is back, "voiceless" now and "thin" as her powers gradually wane; but clearly determined to play at Lorelei from the cliff-tops, teasing and tantalising – as the playful '*v*', '*w*' and '*f*' alliteration suggests. We can even hear the speaker's breathlessness if we give every 'silent h' its traditional pronunciation: "Whither, O whither will its whim now draw me?" This is the kind of line that draws accusations of clumsiness and it is true that the effects are not subtle, but Hardy is merely using broader brush-strokes and brighter oils, a more potently dramatic style than some of his water-colour contemporaries. It is a style that allows him to use (alongside bold choices such as "ejaculations" – at five syllables, by far the longest word in the poem) the simplest diction, though often within quite sinuous sentences. The tenth and eleventh lines, for example, are entirely monosyllabic ("Through the years, through the dead scenes I have tracked you;/What have you now found to say of our past?") and the poem as a whole makes powerful use of such short words, often cunningly phrased and punctuated or shaped in memorably unexpected ways. So, "Things were not lastly as firstly well" (a kind of lovers' baby-talk here) and "At the then fair hour in the then fair weather".

The chosen stanza form is the most substantial of the entire sequence: eight alternately indented lines, opening and closing with pentameter (although only sporadically iambic) and composed in a metre which seems to owe as much to song as traditional prosody: essentially five beats to a line (the last inclining to six), with a trimeter (three beat) penultimate line. Hardy liked to write to a tune in his head, as with his poem inspired by a movement of a Mozart symphony: how sad it is that there is not a single recording of him reciting, whereas we can hear many of the well-known Georgians and even Browning and Tennyson waxing lyrical from their cylinders. What we can imagine is Hardy walking and speaking the lines to a Schubertian pulse as he goes. I have already mentioned that he would often have a clear idea of the rhythm but not the words, even leaving blanks to fill in later. There is a musical imperative in these poems: Hardy doesn't just have something to say, but something to sing, though there may be on the face of it "little cause for carolling".

Like many of the *Poems of 1912–13*, 'After a Journey' depends on juxtaposition of life as it is and life as it was (a technique that would prove essential to First World War poets such as Sassoon, who admired Hardy above all other poets). This contrast provides the template for the stylistic oddities quoted at the end of my first paragraph, but it threads the poem: "Summer gave us sweets, but autumn wrought division?" (note the mournful assonance); "I am just the same as when/Our days were a joy, and our paths through flowers." It could be argued that this concluding line of the poem is rather too easily sentimental, that the rhyme with "though Life lours" offered too much of a temptation. Having walked to Pentargan Bay myself, I am inclined to allow Hardy this indulgence: the paths are veritable tunnels of thrift, trefoil, vetch, daisy ... Besides, flowers have become a crucial element in the sequence, linking the live Emma (lover of daisies) with the dead Emma (flowers on her grave).

The poem as a whole seems to owe something to *A Midsummer Night's Dream*: lovers led into entanglements, hidden fairy powers, flower-magic, playful spite ("I see what you are doing" – itself an echo of Bottom's words, "this is to make an ass of me ...") ... At the end, the poet emerges from his haunted wood, half aware that he has been wearing an ass's head, in the full knowledge that he has known a brief, but enduring, passion. The detail of his return to normality is exquisite:

> Ignorant of what there is flitting here to see,
>   The waked birds preen and the seals flop lazily;
> Soon you will have, Dear, to vanish from me,
>   For the stars close their shutters and the dawn
>   whitens hazily.
> Trust me, I mind not, though Life lours,
>   The bringing me here; nay, bring me here again!

As in 'At Castle Boterel', nature is insensitive to the momentousness of the scene – birds "preen", seals "flop" – and Hardy feels a sudden suburbanisation of the universe (those "shutters"), an uncertainty even in the daybreak ("hazily") by comparison with these Metaphysical lovers, who have created a certain, joyful universe of their own.

XIV A Death-Day Recalled

Hardy now takes the convention of the classical elegy "in which features or places of nature familiar to the dead are personified as mourners" (Bailey) and – typically – turns it on its head. At the moment of Emma's death, when one might have expected some pathetic fallacy, Beeny Cliff and the headland above Boscastle Harbour are both unmoved, there is no symbolic dark cloud over St Juliot, the River Vallency trickles on with perfect callousness, and the breakers continue curling towards Pentargan Bay. Hardy adopts a strict trochaic and alliterative metre to express this (a considerable challenge in so iambic a language as English), enabling him to assert with greater anger the stony indifference of Emma's beloved homeland. The stressed syllables are in italics below:

> *Bee*ny *did* not *qui*ver,
> *Ju*liot *grew* not *gray*,
> *Thin* Vallency's *ri*ver
> *Held* its *won*ted *way*.
> *Bos* seemed *not* to *ut*ter
> *Dim*mest *note* of *dirge*,
> *Tar*gan *mouth* a *mut*ter
> *To* its *crea*my *surge*.

The anger is set aside in the middle stanza and a more melancholy, less emphatically trochaic, mood of reminiscence takes over. In the third the original minor key returns, this time for a series of infuriated questions ("Why did not ... deplore ... thunder ...?"). As a study of grieving, this is perceptive; there is always an element of rage in the process. The poem's structure resembles a scherzo and trio, but more Mahler than Mozart.

'A Death-Day Recalled', of course, tells us nothing of the events at Max Gate on the morning of 27th November. For this, we must look to Hardy's letters and Florence's *Life*. The poem is a decent enough piece of work in its context, but not without its infelicities: the first half of the last stanza is rather tortuous in its quest for a rhyme with Vallency, although the detail is accurate in that the river's source was indeed not far from Emma's house. The wonderfully named Vallency Valley features in several other important poems not included in *Poems of 1912–13*, most memorably 'Under the Waterfall' – the incident of the dropped drinking-glass, which Tom captured in a pencil sketch.

The Valency (as it is spelt these days) by no means always holds "its wonted way" and Hardy might have been interested to know that on 16th August 2004, just before the catastrophic flooding of Boscastle, at least one woman (a volunteer in the Witchcraft Museum) did feel that the place was trying to tell her something. It didn't quite "quiver" or utter a "note of dirge", but, as she described it later, "it was like somebody blew down my bare arms, either side of me, at one particular point" and she even commented on this to the owner. The area, then, may not be entirely "unheeding,/Listless", and Hardy rather confirms this in his own celebration of its "wild weird western shore" in the following poem.

XV Beeny Cliff

As if to remind us that this sequence is not just a display of grief, but a *tour de force* of the poet's metrical prowess, Hardy employs a longer line than usual in groups of three, rhyming *aaa,* with an iambic rhythm tending to the anapaestic, with occasional clusters of stressed syllables at crucial moments: "loved so", "loved me", "sweet things said", "laugh there never ..." Essentially, they are what is known as 'fourteeners': a very old ballad metre. Each stanza of 'Beeny Cliff' is numbered in Roman numerals, corresponding to the five acts of a Shakespearian tragedy. There is little characterisation, but an operatic expression of human vulnerability – protagonists dwarfed by the stage set, the lighting, the sound, their story starkly clear. The effect is unforgettably powerful.

Hardy's opening metre immediately calls attention to the sea's appearance ("O the *op*al and the *sapph*ire"), the way it looks illusively enduring and tangibly precious. Shakespeare's Feste would have pointed out, in addition, that the opal is a symbol of vicissitude. Nothing endures, yet the description is perfectly precise, as a 21st-century walk along the cliff-tops above Boscastle still makes plain. The reader may be puzzled by the opening image of the "wandering western sea", but the walker will see what Hardy meant: one minute the sea is visible, the next it has gone; suddenly it veers in front, then it yawns below. Gulls that should be above are seen below; the sea becomes "a nether sky". It is indeed a coast both wild and "weird" – an adjective whose origins suggest the pagan force of destiny.

At the heart of 'Beeny Cliff' is a key-change: no longer the cheerily alliterative joys and meaningful caesura of the first stanza ("The woman whom I loved so, and who loyally loved me"), Emma Gifford's hair flapping as the pony carries her towards the inaccessible beauty spot. The change is anticipated in the seagulls' solitary monk-chant (three heavy stresses on "pale mews plained" – with a pun or two thrown in) and the odd dream-like effect of distant waves. Sounds, as well as sights, do strange things on the cliffs. Hardy's description implies that "babbling" nature is trivial, transitory, irrelevant beside the lofty timelessness of Tom and Emma's 'Act II'. It is in the third stanza that a very small shift in the weather conditions reminds us that all will not be quite so idyllic in the marriage (Hardy subtitles 'Beeny Cliff' '*March 1870–March 1913*'), but that theirs is to be a colourful relationship, one that calls for very special and precise words: the "irised rain", the "dull misfeatured stain" are briefly reminiscent of a bitter early poem, 'Neutral Tones'. The poet is reminding his readers that he knows "the then fair hour" would not last; but he seems reassured by the fact that the couple knew nothing of that at the time.

What Hardy finds hardest to accept is that he will not now be able to revisit Beeny and revive some of that early passion with Emma – what in our own time would have become a renewal of vows. His 'Act IV' is a heartbroken aria, rich in pulsing monosyllables of disbelief, the adjective "chasmal" echoing the depths of his despair, the verb "bulks" suggesting immovable mockery of human emotions. Both words also capture exactly the physical make-up of this most striking stretch of coast:

> – Still in all its chasmal beauty bulks old Beeny to
> the sky,
> And shall she and I not go there once again now
> March is nigh,
> And the sweet things said in that March say anew
> there by and by?'

Hardy's final stroke of genius is the sudden pause and euphemism in the penultimate line of his fifth Act. Whether because Emma still seems so 'living', or out of respect for her own faith, or the vestiges of his own, he cannot bring himself to say 'dead', substituting: "the woman now is – elsewhere." Beeny Cliff remains to mock this aged widower as he mutters his fourteeners; but the only echo of their shared laughter, of Emma's own laugh is in these lines. Of course, Hardy does not call her Emma: she is "the woman", a Muse, a masked universal figure, something she probably would not have found amusing – certainly Florence Hardy didn't, who seldom laughed at anything.

XVI At Castle Boterel

Another celebrated poem in which place and poetry merge seamlessly, 'At Castle Boterel' describes one of the poet's earliest jaunts with Emma to what the 'real' world knows as Boscastle. The elements are at work here again, though not the energising cliff-top airs of earlier pieces. Hardy's return visit to the picture-postcard harbour is a heavier, wearier affair "amid the rain", emphasising the contrast between his own present misery (note the mood of the third stanza) and the "dry March weather" of past love. The "primeval rocks" are cold recording presences. And there is fire hidden in that repeated word "alight" (seldom used except by poets and transport companies): this poet knows what he means when he says, "that night/Saw us alight."

The focus of Hardy's remembering is their attempt to climb straight up from the harbour, past the grassy site of 'Bottreaux Castle', to the main part of the village, using what is now the old road (access these days is via a winding, more coach-friendly route). It is a long, steep climb and it is hardly surprising that the couple "alighted" from the "chaise" to "ease the sturdy pony's load". J.O. Bailey (in *The Poetry of Thomas Hardy*) wonders whether the couple had made the visit with Emma's sister so that stepping down from the chaise gave them an unchaperoned moment "out of Mrs Holder's sight". These details, particularly after the epic scene-painting of 'Beeny Cliff', give the poem a warmly human dimension, and this is Hardy's point – that the love of these two very ordinary young people in 1840, sightseeing, talking of forgotten everyday matters, is in the end more significant than anything in *Principles of Geology*, published a few years before. Whatever Sir Charles Lyell's work might have led to in terms of Darwinism, religious doubt and Victorian unease, Hardy's personal experience of true love remains momentous and unchanging:

> Primeval rocks form the road's steep border,
> And much have they faced there, first and last,
> Of the transitory in Earth's long order;
> But what they record in colour and cast
> Is – that we two passed.

The choice of this image is as brilliant as its placing within the poem, coming just after the stanza in which Hardy shrugs, "It filled but a minute", and then allows himself an outburst of regret – an apparently rhetorical question ("But was there ever/A time of such quality, since or before,/In that hill's story?") to which he retorts in four plain words ("To one mind never").

From this point on, 'Time' with a capital T dominates the poem. It is "unflinching" and "mindless", doing what it must, having "ruled from sight" the one person Tom loved – a metaphor suggesting a ruthless accountant as much as a despot. The poet himself becomes something out of *Alice in*

Wonderland, "shrinking, shrinking", rhyming himself with a very conventional hour-glass ("my sand is sinking") and flinging out a self-pitying note in the last short line. These brief stanza-ends have been in place throughout the poem, suggesting a breathlessness ("Distinctly yet"), an inevitable curtailment ("When he sighed and slowed"), the sense that life ticks on like a machine ("By thousands more"), but above all Fate waiting round the corner ready to cut things short. 'At Castle Boterel''s elaborate stanza form never imposes itself on the poem's emotions, always heightens and tautens them; it is the poet working at full throttle.

Climbing that same hill today "foot-swift, foot-sore", running fingers over those same folds of slate embedded with fossils, little is added to or taken from Hardy's masterpiece, but one has the feeling that his point is conclusively made – perhaps all the more poignantly since a good deal of the town he and Emma visited was washed away in 2004. But the Wellington Hotel, where he stayed, survived. And one can still buy from the reconstructed visitor centre Heulyn and Ginny Lewis' excellent little *In the Footsteps of Thomas and Emma Hardy*. That story simply cannot be erased.

XVII Places

Not the strongest of the *Poems of 1912–13*, 'Places' depends rather too heavily on biographical details about Emma, plundering her memoir, *Some Recollections*, to little memorable effect. Its four-stanza structure follows a sequence of three negatives ("Nobody says ...", "Nobody thinks ...", "Nobody calls to mind ..."), offset by the poet's final resolution – "Nay: one there is to whom these things ...Have a savour ..." What 'Nobody' notices at first concerns Emma's early life in Plymouth – evoked somewhat conventionally and sentimentally ("a little girl of grace –/ The sweetest the house saw ..." "like the bud of a flower") – where the "stammering chimes" heard by the girl as she lies in bed are the only interesting detail in two stanzas. The third returns us to Boscastle and the steepness of its hill, but Hardy's imagery of skidding waggoners and rosy-cheeked fearlessness, while it would undoubtedly have pleased Emma, pales in the dazzle of 'At Castle Boterel'. The disillusionment that crept into that poem recurs in the final image of 'Places', where contemporary life is seen (with characteristically lively diction) as "beneaped and stale,/ And its urgent clack/But a vapid tale." This stanza salvages the poem – just! – with its attention to the idea that memory can be more potent and real than "the actual".

XVIII The Phantom Horsewoman

The final 'movement' of the suite begins with cantering rhythms, well captured by the composer Gerald Finzi in his setting for *Earth and Air and Rain*. Again, Hardy invents a stanza form that suits his purposes: tetrameter (four-beat) lines to start and finish, rhyming *aa* – the rhymes separated by seven dimeter (two-beat) lines, themselves rhyming *bcbcbca*, and sufficiently fast-paced still to echo the opening. Because 'The Phantom Horsewoman' introduces a new narrative voice, this structure enables Hardy to juxtapose the narrator's commentary with description of what he sees. The surprise in finding that we are no longer in the poet's company, but observing him from afar through a stranger's eyes, prepares us for a change in mood, for a distancing, although by the end, the narrator has guessed fairly accurately what the poet is imagining and feeling.

After the blandness of 'Places', Hardy is back on form. His focus is very much on memory and loss, their effect on personality. The scenery has receded to a "seaward haze ... briny green", most vividly (in our last glimpse of the Cornish coast) as "that shagged and shaly/Atlantic spot". The scrutinising passer-by, like a film camera panning, then zooming in, observes from a distance the "careworn craze" of the odd man who keeps staring out to sea. It is only as we are drawn in from long-shot to medium-shot and the "moveless hands/And face and gaze" that we recognise that this is Hardy, so the voice we are hearing cannot be his. If this were indeed a film, there would be a steady close-up of the poet in profile against the waves as we hear the words of the second stanza: what "they say he sees". There would probably be a flashback ("a sweet soft scene" – did Hardy know about soft-focus techniques?) to capture the Blakean essence of the echoing past "By that briny green"; then some kind of special effect to introduce the "phantom of his own figuring".

The ghost, then, has made a last appearance; but now it is seen at second-hand, distantly, and we are assured that it is purely imagined ("own figuring ... this vision"), and the narrator implies that this is taken as evidence of his craziness ("Not only there/Does he see this sight/But everywhere"). Hardy's self-mockery is touching. If we had not already guessed, the fourth stanza opens with the revelation of what it is (they say) he sees: "A ghost-girl-rider". "Riding became her passion," Claire Tomalin tells us, explaining how Emma was kindly given a mare by her sister's employer, "and she was off, cantering about Cornwall on her own, happily and fearlessly." Hardy was altogether impressed by her equestrian skills when he first met her. Tomalin reminds us that Emma had been born with a limp, so riding would always be a particular pleasure (later it would be the "byke"). Music, too, was one of her delights and – something Finzi highlights in his setting – she leaves the poem singing "to the swing of the tide". If Hardy had read Gerard Manley Hopkins, which is possible as his own late poetry seems to bear his influence, he would have known 'Heaven-Haven: *A nun takes the veil*', with its final image of release: "Where the green swell is in the havens dumb,/ And out of the swing of the sea".

XIX The Spell of the Rose

'The Phantom Horsewoman' was originally to have ended the sequence, but Hardy decided to add a further three poems, "more distanced and desolate" as Rosenthal and Gall put it. Keen to maintain variety in the sequence, and to suggest their love story becoming part of the fabric of tradition, Hardy adopts a ballad form and an allegorical theme, giving the main narrative voice to a woman. It works well enough within its context, but it is not quite the kind of poetry Hardy is comfortable with. Having echoed Hopkins in the last poem, now he sounds rather like the Yeats of 'Innisfree', 'Aengus' or 'Cap and Bells'. The lover describes the grand hall he wishes to build (very unlike Max Gate, although the words are those Tom used when planning it), planted with "roses love shall feed upon". In true ballad style, this sequence of wishes is repeated by the beloved ("He built for me that manor-hall,/And planted many trees withal,/But no rose anywhere"), with a privately sardonic touch to that "many trees", since they were one of Hardy's distracting "June-time" passions, though they came to "obscure the sky". In the third stanza the woman attributes the subsequent "horrid shows" in their relationship to the lack of these loving roses. She decides (with Giffordian independence of spirit) to "mend these miseries", and creeps out by night to plant one. Inevitably, she dies before the rose can flourish, "And would that now I knew/What feels he of the tree I planted,/And whether, after I was called/To be a ghost, he, as of old,/Gave me his heart anew." She imagines what we have already seen happening in the poems: the man who forgot about love at last seeing what he missed when she was alive: "He sees me as I was, though sees/Too late to tell me so!"

XX St Launce's Revisited

Moving us back towards Dorset, where the sequence began, Hardy stops off at Launceston (associated in most poetry-readers' minds with that child of Hardy, a poet with an equally common touch, the late Charles Causley), where the railway line ended in 1870. It was from 'St Launce's' that he had "hired a conveyance for the additional sixteen or seventeen miles' distance by the Boscastle road towards the north coast"; forty-three years later he is there again, adding to the tradition of English 'revisited' poems. He addresses "Time" directly, rhyming it with "prime" as he often likes to. There is a curt, hopeless quality to the writing (short lines, abrupt enjambments) resisting any lyrical impulses. The "gray" castle and the gloomy inn ("jade" rather than horse; his hosts "strange") contrast with the fantastic grandeur of the "hall" in the ballad we have just read. Emma is nowhere to be seen, not even an allegorical Emma, or ghost-girl-rider Emma. He is preoccupied by the original journey that was to begin here and take him to the "dwelling" of the rectory at St Juliot – a building far from gloomy or grey or baronial, a true "domicilium". The poem ends with an attempt to recapture the enthusiasm ("If again/ Towards the Atlantic sea there/I should speed, they'd be there/Surely now as then? ...") but this falters into self-disgust and depression, the rhymes guttering out: "thought ... vanished ... banished ... nought".

XXI Where the Picnic Was

The story ends once again by the sea, but this time it is almost certainly (and symmetry demands it) the Dorset coast. There have been those who think we are still in Cornwall, the 'four' being Hardy, Emma, her sister Helen and her husband, vicar of St Juliot. But the reference to "last year" in the context of the sequence makes 1912 the most likely occasion – the other two perhaps even being Yeats and Newbolt, who came to present Hardy with the gold medal of the Royal Society of Literature. But that had been a somewhat embarrassing occasion (Hardy banished Emma from the room for the ceremony), so this is improbable. It is no doubt a deliberate irony on Hardy's part that although he gave the poem such a precise title, and while every other location in a sequence dominated by place is identifiable, "where the picnic was" is unknown to the most learned critics. Like Elgar (with whom he almost collaborated), Thomas Hardy enjoyed strewing the trail with false leads.

We are once more keeping company with the poet, feeling his age as we "climb/Through winter mire" and he nostalgically tracks down the location of perhaps their last picnic. He (unlike his biographers) finds the place "readily". The poem's diction is unforced, the rhymes natural, with a sense of a speaking voice in the pauses and interjections. The fire of passion is now out and – along with a cold wind and discoloured grass – only a "burnt circle" remains. Curves and straightness are important: Hardy is last relic of the "band" who picnicked here; while the sea makes a "strange straight line". We are reminded of Time's "rule" in 'At Castle Boterel': the ruthless directness of fate, contrasted with the meandering deliciousness of romance on "this grassy rise". That image connects, sadly, with grave-mounds, and the poet is soon remembering (with a presciently eco-conscious touch) that "two have wandered far/From this grassy rise/Into urban roar/Where no picnics are,/And one – has shut her eyes/For evermore." It is a fine poem, a fitting and understated finale, the sequence having itself come full circle.

Bibliography

Below is a list of relevant books referred to in the text.

The standard edition of Hardy's poetry is *The Complete Poems*, New Wessex Edition (Macmillan, 1976) edited by James Gibson, although there are several decent alternatives and innumerable substantial selections. Not all of them include the full sequence, *Poems of 1912–13*. The *Letters* are available in an edition by Michael Millgate and R.L. Purdy.

Criticism
J.O. Bailey, *The Poetry of Thomas Hardy: A Handbook and Commentary* (University of North Carolina Press, 1970).
Donald Davie, *Thomas Hardy and British Poetry* (Routledge & Kegan Paul, 1973).
James Gibson and Trevor Johnson, *Thomas Hardy: Poems* Casebook Series (Macmillan, 1979).
Philip Larkin, *Required Writing* (Faber, 1983) and *The Oxford Book of Twentieth-Century English Verse* (OUP, 1973).
F.R. Leavis, *New Bearings in English Poetry* (Chatto & Windus, 1932).
M.L. Rosenthal and Sally M. Gall, *The Modern Poetic Sequence* (OUP, 1986).

Biographies
Robert Gittings, *Young Thomas Hardy* and *The Older Hardy* (Penguin, 1975/8)
Emma Hardy, *Some Recollections* (OUP, 1961).

Florence Hardy, *The Early Life* and *The Later Years* (1928/
30) reissued as *The Life of Thomas Hardy* (1962), then
'outed' as *The Life and Work of Thomas Hardy* (1984) by
Hardy himself.

F.E. Halliday, *Thomas Hardy, His Life and Work* (Granada,
1978).

Heulyn and Ginny Lewis, *In the Footsteps of Thomas and
Emma Hardy* (The North Cornwall Coast and Country-
side Service, 2003).

Michael Millgate, *Thomas Hardy: A Critical Biography*
(Oxford University Press, 1982).

Martin Seymour-Smith, *Hardy* (Bloomsbury, 1994).

Claire Tomalin, *Thomas Hardy, The Time-Torn Man*
(Penguin, 2006).

Music

Gerald Finzi, *Earth and Air and Rain*, Roderick Williams
& Iain Burnside (Naxos, 2006).

GREENWICH EXCHANGE BOOKS

STUDENT GUIDE LITERARY SERIES

The Greenwich Exchange Student Guide Literary Series is a collection of essays on major or contemporary serious writers in English and selected European languages. The series is for the student, the teacher and 'common readers' and is an ideal resource for libraries. The *Times Educational Supplement* praised these books, saying, "The style of [this series] has a pressure of meaning behind it. Readers should learn from that ... If art is about selection, perception and taste, then this is it."

(ISBN prefix 978-1-871551 applies unless marked*, when the prefix 978-1-906075 applies.)

The series includes:
Antonin Artaud by Lee Jamieson (98-3)
W.H. Auden by Stephen Wade (36-5)
Honoré de Balzac by Wendy Mercer (48-8)
William Blake by Peter Davies (27-3)
The Brontës by Peter Davies (24-2)
Robert Browning by John Lucas (59-4)
Lord Byron by Andrew Keanie (83-9)
Samuel Taylor Coleridge by Andrew Keanie (64-8)
Joseph Conrad by Martin Seymour-Smith (18-1)
William Cowper by Michael Thorn (25-9)
Charles Dickens by Robert Giddings (26-9)
Emily Dickinson by Marnie Pomeroy (68-6)
John Donne by Sean Haldane (23-5)
Ford Madox Ford by Anthony Fowles (63-1)
The Stagecraft of Brian Friel by David Grant (74-7)
Robert Frost by Warren Hope (70-9)
Patrick Hamilton by John Harding (99-0)
Thomas Hardy by Sean Haldane (33-4)
Seamus Heaney by Warren Hope (37-2)
Joseph Heller by Anthony Fowles (84-6)
Gerard Manley Hopkins by Sean Sheehan (77-3)
James Joyce by Michael Murphy (73-0)
Philip Larkin by Warren Hope (35-8)
Laughter in the Dark – The Plays of Joe Orton by Arthur Burke (56-3)
George Orwell by Warren Hope (42-6)
Sylvia Plath by Marnie Pomeroy (88-4)